IMAGES
of America

INDEPENDENCE HALL
AND THE LIBERTY BELL

Looking northeast, this aerial view of the old Pennsylvania State House Yard, now known as Independence Square, was taken from atop the Penn Mutual Building on March 21, 1929. The image gives a historic perspective of the way Philadelphia appeared in the 1920s. It also reveals how Independence Hall easily blended into the city's skyline. By 1730, the Pennsylvania Legislature had finally purchased all the lots necessary to start construction of the Pennsylvania State House on a city block that is bounded by Chestnut, Fifth, Walnut, and Sixth Streets. The location at that time was viewed as being on the outskirts of town, as the city developed along the banks of the Delaware River and eventually began to grow westward. Over the decades, the "City of Brotherly Love" rose around the Colonial structure. In the 1950s, Independence Mall would be created by razing all the buildings within a three-block area to create an open vista of Independence Hall. Today, Independence Hall is the central focus of Independence National Historical Park. (INHP.)

ON THE COVER: On September 12, 1919, Gen. John J. Pershing was honored in Philadelphia with possibly one of the largest parades the city had ever given to a war hero. The streets along the parade route were decorated with flowers and American flags. Even Independence Hall was adorned for the general's visit. Young ladies dressed in costumes representing each Allied nation that participated in World War I stand by the Liberty Bell. (INHP.)

IMAGES
of America

INDEPENDENCE HALL
AND THE LIBERTY BELL

Robert W. Sands Jr. and
Alexander B. Bartlett

ARCADIA
PUBLISHING

Published by Arcadia Publishing
Charleston, South Carolina

Printed in the United States of America

Library of Congress Control Number: 2011945126

For all general information, please contact Arcadia Publishing:
Telephone 843-853-2070
Fax 843-853-0044
E-mail sales@arcadiapublishing.com
For customer service and orders:
Toll-Free 1-888-313-2665

Visit us on the Internet at www.arcadiapublishing.com

This 1906 vintage postcard depicting John Trumbull's painting titled *Declaration of Independence* was commissioned in 1817. (CA.)

CONTENTS

Acknowledgments

The publication of this book would not have been possible without the assistance of many people. With extreme thanks and appreciation, we would like to acknowledge the following: Christian Higgins and Andrea Ashby of the Independence National Historical Park Archives who were extremely helpful providing information, insight, and images. Special thanks to Andrea for her guidance, direction, and support. We could not have asked for more and are indebted to her for her kindness. To Deb Boyer, of PhillyHistory.org; Brenda Galloway and her staff at the Urban Archives of Temple University; Aurora Deshauteurs, curator of the Print and Picture Collection; Virginia Grier of the Philadelphia Free Library Newspaper and Microfilm Center; and Kenneth R. Speth. We would like to thank our friends, colleagues, and family for their never-ending patience and support. Lastly, we would like to express our gratitude to Alexandra and Stephen Bartlett and William C. Mitchell for your love and support. Thank you!

We would like to acknowledge the courtesy of the following institutions from whom images were provided: Atlanta History Center (AHC); the Philadelphia History Museum at the Atwater Kent Museum (AKM/PM); Abraham Lincoln Presidential Library and Museum (ALPLM); collection of the authors (CA); Print and Picture Collection, Free Library of Philadelphia (FLP); Gerald R. Ford Presidential Library and Museum (GFPLM); Independence National Historical Park (INHP); Kenneth R. Speth Collection (KS); Library of Congress (LC); Missouri History Museum, St. Louis (MHM); the Massachusetts Historical Society (MHS); the National Aeronautics and Space Administration (NASA); the Pennsylvania Academy of the Fine Arts, Philadelphia, gift of Sarah Harrison (The Joseph Harrison Jr. Collection) (PAFA); PhillyHistory.org, a project of the Philadelphia Department of Records (PH); San Diego History Center (SDHC); Duke University (DU); State Historical Society of Missouri (SHSM); Special Collections Research Center, Temple University Libraries, Philadelphia, Pennsylvania (UA); UPI Photo/Anderson/ Files (UPI); and used with permission of Philadelphia Inquirer Permissions copyright 1959, all rights reserved (YGS).

INTRODUCTION

Independence Hall and the Liberty Bell are two of the most revered symbols of American freedom; the two are forever linked. Although both were relatively overlooked in their early history, their importance and visibility in American history gradually increased. Interestingly enough, when constructed and cast, neither were intended to be the iconic symbols of democracy and liberty that they have become not only for Americans, but for many around the world.

The history of Independence Hall can be divided into four major periods: 1732–1799 serving as the Pennsylvania State House as well as home for the Continental Congress and the Constitutional Convention; 1802–1828 as a museum for Charles Willson Peale; 1818–1895 as the municipal building for the city of Philadelphia; and 1891 to the present as a historic shrine. The interior has been renovated many times, but the exterior remains much the way it appeared when constructed in the early 1730s.

The Liberty Bell, originally known as the Pennsylvania State House Bell, would be given its name "Liberty Bell" by abolitionists who adopted the bell as their symbol in the 1800s. The bell, although it makes no sound, has spoken volumes for many. Between 1885 and 1915, the popularity of the Liberty Bell was heightened as it traveled throughout the United States to be exhibited at several world's fairs and anniversary celebrations. Positioned on the back of a flatbed railcar, the Liberty Bell would make frequent stops along the route, allowing all the opportunity to see, touch, and have a photograph taken of the event.

Independence Hall and the Liberty Bell is a photographic history chronicling the transformation of these two great icons into symbols of individual liberty and freedom. It would have been a great oversight to ignore the many people associated with these cherished symbols of freedom, for people ultimately shaped them into the treasured icons they are today. Politicians, protesters, entertainers, dignitaries, religious figures, workers, students, and tourists all helped to give Independence Hall and the Liberty Bell that glorious historic patina that would have been impossible to achieve without them. And so we have included photographs of these people, to celebrate this achievement.

It is our intent that the photographs within *Independence Hall and the Liberty Bell* will help bring people closer to the rich history that Independence Hall and the Liberty Bell embody. Hopefully this book will contribute to a greater understanding of these symbols of freedom and will help to ensure their presence on the historic landscape for generations to come.

The City of Philadelphia still retains ownership of Independence Hall and the Liberty Bell. Both are maintained by the National Park Service, but in spirit, they are owned by the world.

Philadelphians brave a winter storm as they walk through Independence Square on January 29, 1925. "Philadelphia faces the heaviest snowfall of the winter," began an article in *The Evening Bulletin*. Temperatures dropped to 15 degrees in the early morning hours, which made for the coldest January 29 in Philadelphia since 1885. Overnight, four inches of snow fell over the city with high winds. The fluctuation of temperatures caused snow to turn to rain and back to snow again. Transportation through the region was met with slippery roads and clogged trolley tracks. As of that date, 11.2 inches of snow had fallen in Philadelphia for the month of January 1925. (UA.)

One

INDEPENDENCE HALL,
THE BIRTHPLACE OF A NATION

Independence Hall is an American landmark that is recognized around the world. Constructed as the Pennsylvania State House in 1732, three of America's most important documents, the Declaration of Independence, Articles of Confederation, and the Constitution were drafted in this building. The structure has become a shrine to the principles of freedom and democracy. A National Park Service guide answers questions outside Independence Hall in 1959. (INHP.)

Andrew Hamilton was a Philadelphia attorney of Scottish descent. He is credited as being the guiding force behind the construction of Independence Hall. Less than two years after William Penn granted the Charter of Privileges, the Pennsylvania Assembly became the most powerful and independent Colonial legislature in America. Meeting in private homes and taverns, Hamilton, speaker of the Pennsylvania Assembly, felt strongly that the assembly should have a dignified place to meet. (CA.)

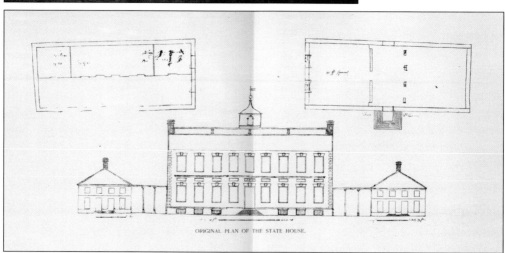

ORIGINAL PLAN OF THE STATE HOUSE.

Members of the Pennsylvania Assembly, along with Andrew Hamilton, began to purchase lots on Chestnut Street by October 1730. Architect Edmund Woolley is credited for designing and constructing Independence Hall. Construction began in 1732. Due to a lack of funding, the construction was done piecemeal and was completed in 1753. This sketch is the original plan for the Pennsylvania State House, which would later be known as Independence Hall. (CA.)

When the Pennsylvania State House was constructed, two arched piazzas bridged two adjacent structures on the east and west side of the main building. These archways were enclosed on the south side and contained a staircase connecting the main building with the second floors of each wing. This is noticeable in this 1776 engraving of Independence Hall by John C. McRae. (FLP.)

This c. 1799 engraving of Independence Hall by William Birch shows the belfry removed from the tower and covered with a hipped roof. By 1773, the tower had deteriorated to a dangerous level. In 1781, it was removed by order of the Pennsylvania Assembly. The present belfry was designed in 1828 by American architect William Strickland. The new design of the steeple included a clock and used more ornamentation. (FLP.)

In 1812, the City of Philadelphia was given permission by the state to demolish the original wings and piazzas and replace them with new fireproof offices. Robert Mills designed the structures in keeping with Philadelphia's early-19th-century streetscape of row houses. Mills's design incorporated characteristic elements from Independence Hall—a brick facade and keystones. These structures adjoined both Old City Hall and Congress Hall. (CA.)

Independence Hall, seen around 1875 looking east on Chestnut Street, shows the west portion of the Mills buildings. Many of Philadelphia's city government offices were located here. Among them were the recorder of deeds and the sheriff's office. The office signs are visible above the doors. As part of a restoration project in 1897, the structures were torn down and replaced with incorrectly proportioned imitations of the 1735 structures. (CA.)

This c. 1940 view shows the reconstruction of the east wing of Independence Hall and its piazza. The new wings were not built to the exact proportions of the originals but were constructed slightly larger. They were built during the height of a Colonial revival that occurred in America in the late 1800s. The new wings and piazzas were completed and open to the public on July 4, 1898. (PH.)

The piazzas that bridge between Independence Hall and both east and west wings are replicas of the originals that were constructed in the 1730s. The piazzas along with the wings were removed in 1812 to construct the Mills buildings. These buildings were occupied by municipal offices when Independence Hall operated as Philadelphia's city hall. In 1898, the Mills buildings were removed and both wings and archways reconstructed. (INHP.)

This shows the Stretch Clock reconstruction project along the west wall of Independence Hall in 1962. By order of the Pennsylvania Assembly, two clocks were placed on the east and west walls of the state house. In 1753, local clockmaker Thomas Stretch was put in charge of the construction. When a new clock was added to the tower of the state house, the Stretch Clock became no more than ornamentation. (INHP.)

This is the reinstallation of the Stretch Clock in 1972, on the west wall of Independence Hall. The Stretch Clock remained on the wall until around 1830. It was removed to construct the Mills buildings, which were attached to both sides of Independence Hall. Around 1914, the clock was replaced with a dummy face, which did not operate. It was later removed. It would take nearly 10 years to restore the clock to its current splendor. (CA.)

Two youngsters enjoy a bicycle ride through Independence Square in this early-1870s stereopticon view. The image gives a different perspective of the Mills buildings constructed in 1812 and flanking both ends of Independence Hall. What is not easily noticed is the wrought-iron fence that once enclosed the back portion of the buildings. There appears to be very little exterior change to the building. (CA.)

A firefighting demonstration was staged at Independence Hall on June 21, 1937. The demonstration was performed for delegates of an annual convention of the National Association of Insurance Commissioners. A variety of historic and present-day equipment was used to demonstrate effective firefighting techniques. The demonstration showed how two heavy streams of water can be poured over Independence Hall within two and a half minutes after an alarm is sounded. (INIIP.)

This photograph of Independence Hall and surrounding structures was taken in 1910 from the roof of the American Philosophical Society, offering a good perspective of how the urban landscape surrounded the historic landmark. The neighborhood was considered urban blight and threatened the security of Independence Hall. In 1948, Independence National Historical Park was created. Soon city and state officials approved plans to create a park within the three blocks north of Independence Hall. In 1950, the acquisition and demolition of 143 buildings began in the first block north between Chestnut and Market Streets and proceeded north towards Race Street. The clearing of these blocks would take nine years and was completed in 1959. Now known as Independence Mall, the space has created an open view of Independence Hall and a parklike environment for visitors and residents alike. (LC.)

The construction of Independence Mall began with the demolition of the first block of buildings between Market (foreground) and Chestnut Streets, seen in this November 1951 photograph. City planner Edmund Bacon hired Roy Larson to design the mall. Many of the structures that were being demolished exhibited beautiful 19th-century architecture. Supporters of the mall saw these buildings as eyesores. Merchants along Market Street resisted. (UA.)

In this c. 1953 image, many of the structures along Chestnut Street had been cleared away; however, the project was met with much delay. Merchants who were being evicted were resistant to relocate. Budget problems of the Commonwealth of Pennsylvania, which helped fund the project, caused delays as well as disputes with the demolition company. By late 1953, much of the first block was cleared of debris. (INHP.)

This is a 1950 aerial view of Independence Hall with city structures in the background. This view, taken from the Penn Mutual Building, shows the area north of Independence Hall just prior to the demolition of the structures. Independence Hall is in the foreground, with Independence Square at the bottom of the photograph. This view illustrates the closed-in feeling of Independence Hall in relation to its surroundings. In 1946, the city and state allocated an initial $3 million for the project. (INHP.)

This is an aerial view of Independence Hall with Independence Mall in the background, taken in 2004. The openness of the mall allows for a parklike environment as a backdrop for Independence Hall but provides an open space for a highly developed commercial area. Visible in the picture are, from left to right, (first row) cupola of Congress Hall, Independence Hall, and cupola of Old City Hall; (second row) Liberty Bell Center and old Liberty Bell Pavilion; (third row) Independence Visitor Center and National Constitution Center. (CA.)

All in a day's work, these courageous men dangle from atop the steeple of Independence Hall armed with ladders and paintbrushes in this 1922 photograph. The steeple spire, which was reconstructed in 1828 by William Strickland, rises 168 feet, 7¼ inches above the ground. The tower has been an exceedingly hard portion of the building to maintain. In recent years, the tower has been reinforced with steel beams. (INHP.)

Masons repair mortar between brickwork atop the south end chimneys of Independence Hall in 1941. This portion of the building appears in the fictional movie *National Treasure*, produced by Walt Disney Productions in 2004. It is here that Benjamin Gates, played by actor Nicolas Cage, discovers a pair of multicolor glasses created by Benjamin Franklin that reveals additional clues on the back of the Declaration of Independence. (PH.)

During a major restoration project throughout the National Park known as Mission 66, Independence Hall was a recipient. The steeple had undergone a major reconstruction. Steel reinforcements were installed to stabilize the inner structure. Surveyors measure portions of the tower in preparation for this work in 1962. (LC.)

A $4.3 million renovation project of the tower of Independence Hall began in July 2010. The 14-month-long project included replacing water-damaged structural beams and refurbishing selected deteriorated features of the tower, which was reconstructed in 1828. Large scrims with the image of the tower covered the scaffolding that would affect the appearance of the structure for visitors to the park. The scrims were funded by the Friends of Independence National Historical Park. (CA.)

Two

INSIDE THE HALL OF INDEPENDENCE

The entry hall of Independence Hall is seen here as it appeared in the 1930s. The detailing and overall feel of the architecture set the tone for the rest of the building. It is meant to impress upon visitors that the structure is an important one. The presence of the Liberty Bell reinforced this message and helped to connect Independence Hall and the bell as two icons of American freedom. (CA.)

The Assembly Room, also known as the Signers Room, is seen as it appeared after restoration in 1913. Many of the objects that appear in the room were connected to the signing of the Declaration of Independence and the United States Constitution. In 1854, many of the portraits in the room were created by artist Charles Willson Peale and purchased by the City of Philadelphia at a public auction. (CA.)

This is a view of the entrance to the Assembly Room in 1931. At this time, the Assembly Room was not furnished to resemble the period of time the Continental Congress occupied this room. In 1928, Independence Hall curator Wilfred Jordan began to research the design and construction of the furnishings, assisted by the American Institute of Architects in order to depict an accurate representation of the room during the signing of the Declaration of Independence. (INHP.)

Members the Philadelphia Bar Association reenacted the signing of the Declaration of Independence for a television program that aired July 3, 1951. The skit was performed in the Assembly Room for the 175th anniversary of the United States' independence. The cast are, from left to right, Harold D. Saylor, Howard M. Kuehner, Richard P. Brown, Albert C. Weymann Jr., Bertram K. Wolfe, Raymond A. Speiser, and James B. Anderson. (INHP.)

The Assembly Room in this 1969 photograph, taken by George Eisenman, depicts the room as it may have appeared at the time of the signing of the Declaration of Independence. In 1967, the Murphy, Quigley Company of Bala Cynwyd, Pennsylvania, an interior alterations and renovations company, was selected by the National Park Service to restore the Assembly Room to its original condition. (LC.)

In this rare c. 1870 view of the Assembly Room, objects of the nation's independence fill the space. In 1855, the room became the portrait gallery for many of Charles Willson Peale's oil paintings of Colonial and Revolutionary figures. These can be seen hanging on the back wall. The life-size statue of George Washington was created by William Rush in 1815. Today, these portraits and the Washington statue are on display at the Second Bank of the United States. On the right, the Liberty Bell is seen resting upon a large pedestal, surrounded by liberty caps. The bell, which had been hidden from public view for nearly 100 years, was placed in the room around 1852. Perched atop the Liberty Bell is an American bald eagle, presented by Charles Willson Peale, who operated his museum on the second floor of the building in the early 1800s. To the left, placed upon the Signers Desk, is the Rising Sun Chair, which was used by George Washington during the Constitutional Convention of 1787. (CA.)

The Syng inkstand, created by Philadelphia silversmith Philip Syng in 1752, was used during the signing of the Declaration of Independence and the United States Constitution. It is considered one of the few remaining objects present at the Constitutional Convention. The inkstand was moved to Harrisburg and used by the Pennsylvania Legislature. It was returned to Philadelphia in 1875 and is currently displayed in the West Wing of Independence Hall. (PH.)

The Rising Sun Chair was given its name by Benjamin Franklin during the Constitutional Convention. Franklin stared at the carved sun on the back of President Washington's chair and was not certain whether the sun was rising or setting. When the convention ended, he realized that it was a rising sun. The chair was sent to the state capital in Harrisburg and returned to Independence Hall in 1875. (UA.)

The Supreme Court Chamber is seen as it appeared c. 1904 after a restoration by architect T. Mellon Rogers in 1896. The two large windows behind the judge's bench were reopened after the demolition of the municipal offices of the Mills buildings. The mosaic tile floor, which was installed 1874–1876, was removed and replaced with wood. A decorative roundel was placed in the center of the ceiling. (LC.)

The Supreme Court Chamber is pictured in 1973 after a major renovation project, known as Mission 66, on Independence Hall in the early 1960s. One of the prominent features in the room is the c. 1785 George Rutter painting of the Pennsylvania Coat of Arms. After the American Revolution, this painting replaced the Royal Coat of Arms that was ultimately destroyed. (LC.)

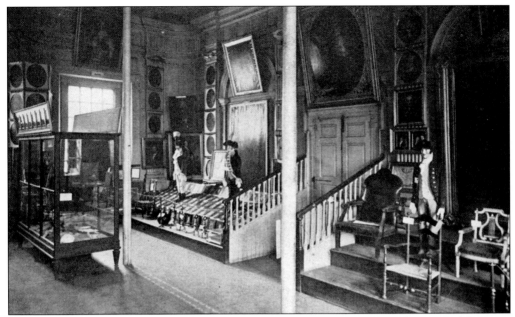

The Supreme Court Chamber is seen as it appeared around 1876, when the function of the room was the National Museum. Many of the objects displayed were relics relating to the American Revolution. Visible on the walls are several of the artworks painted by artist Charles Willson Peale. In 1789, the archways dividing the courtroom and the entry hall were sealed off. Noticeable is the mosaic tiling installed on the floor in 1874–1876. (CA.)

This is a c. 1915 rear view of the Supreme Court Chamber. The room was restored to a Colonial appearance in 1898. The arches over the entryway leading into the courtroom, which was sealed off in 1789, were once again reopened. Visible in the room is the life-size statue of George Washington created by William Rush in 1815. (FLP.)

The West Wing of Independence Hall is seen as it appeared in the 1950s. Many of the structures within the Independence Hall Complex had been utilized as museum space. Climate control was beginning to be considered for the comfort of the visitors. In the 1960s, greater importance was given to the preservation of the objects, with the introduction of air-conditioning. Currently this room is the home of the *Great Essentials* exhibit. (PH.)

This 1822 self-portrait of artist Charles Willson Peale titled *The Artist in His Museum* shows Peale revealing his collection of native biological and archaeological specimens as well as portraits of American heroes and other notables. In 1802, Peale moved to the second floor of Independence Hall after outgrowing his space in the American Philosophical Society. Upon his death in 1827, the museum was sold to showmen P.T. Barnum and Moses Kimball. (PAFA.)

In 1854, Philadelphia County and City merged to create a single municipality, governed by one body. With the suburban communities uniting with Philadelphia City, the population grew from 121,000 to 566,000. The Long Room on the second floor was divided to create two large chambers for the new city government. The windows in the background look out onto Chestnut Street. (INHP.)

The Philadelphia Select Council, seen here in 1893, was part of the legislature branch of city government from 1691 to 1919. The council was responsible for building and maintaining the city's infrastructure. The Select Council was an elected body empowered to choose mayors of the city until 1839. Another executive privilege included the appointment of city officers until 1885. (INHP.)

The Common Council Chamber c. 1895 was the second room constructed from the division of the Long Room. A spectator's gallery extends across the back wall allowing public viewing of council meetings. Interesting features to note are the electric fixtures hanging from the ceiling. Electrical wiring was installed in Independence Hall in 1886. Fourteen fixtures were hung in the Common Council and eight fixtures in the Select Council. (FLP.)

Philadelphia Common Council was formed under the charter created by William Penn in 1691. The council originally consisted of officers of the proprietorship but became an elected governing body in 1789. In 1919, the city charter was revised and the Select and Common Councils combined to form one city council. (INHP.)

The Select Council Chamber is shown c. 1896 during restoration by orders of Philadelphia mayor Edwin S. Stuart. Restoration of the second floor was to covert the room to its earlier appearance. At this time, many city offices and council chambers were relocated to the newly constructed Philadelphia City Hall at Penn Square. The photograph reveals original floorboards that were covered during the 1854 construction of the council chambers. (INHP.)

The Common Council Chamber is shown during restoration c. 1896. The wall constructed to divide the Select and Common Council Chambers was removed to restore the Long Room to its former splendor. The floorboards, which were removed, revealed the previous outline of the former south wall of the Long Room. To the left are the windows that face Chestnut Street. (INHP.)

This is a view of the Long Room shortly after reconstruction by architect T. Mellon Rogers in 1896. Rogers was retained by the Daughters of the American Revolution (DAR), who received permission from the city to restore the second floor at their own expense. Unfortunately, Rogers followed Andrew Hamilton's proposed plans for the Pennsylvania State House rather than the plans used to construct this building, causing an inaccurate reconstruction of the second floor. (INHP.)

In 1922, the Philadelphia chapter of the American Institute of Architects (AIA) sought to correct the inaccurate interpretation of the second floor made during T. Mellon Rogers's 1896 restoration. Not only was his reconstruction of the second floor incorrect, but it conflicted with the architecture of the first floor. Much of the fireplace mantels and door pediments would be completely redone to appear much closer to 18th-century architecture. (INHP.)

The Governor's Council Chamber on the second-floor southwest room of Independence Hall is seen here in 1973. The room depicts the meeting place of the Colonial governor and council before the American Revolution. To avoid misinterpretation, the National Park Service restored the room based on the designs of the pediments above the closet doors to the tower stairway and the entrance to the Assembly Room. (LC.)

The Assembly Committee Chamber on the southeast corner of the second floor is seen here in 1973. The room was used to store munitions by the City of Philadelphia in the early 1770s. The Pennsylvania Assembly occupied the room in 1775, after providing the first-floor room to the Continental Congress. By removing the wall, the room was reconstructed to create the City Council Chamber in 1854. The room was restored in 1896. (LC.)

Shown here is a rare, c. 1895 interior view of the sheriff's office, once located in the west wing of the Mills buildings. Detailed information about the interior of this building is scarce. The cabinets' doors bear the names of former Philadelphia sheriffs (H.P. Connell and William H. Wright, for instance). The sign on the cabinet reads, "On and after June 10th, 1893 this office will close on Saturdays at 12 o'clock." (AKM/PM.)

Private quarters in the sheriff's office in the west wing of the Mills buildings is seen here. The c. 1895 image shows a gate towards the left, which may have separated public and restricted areas. A wash basin, mirror, and water cooler can be seen in the center of the photograph, suggesting that this space may have been designated for personal use. (AKM/PM.)

This is the staircase leading to the clock tower in Independence Hall. This room was once the lodging of Andrew McNair, the caretaker of the Pennsylvania State House during the American Revolution. One of the trusses that held the Liberty Bell is visible in this 1929 image. The room still contains the fireplace with which McNair cooked and provided heat and the remnant of a lightning rod Benjamin Franklin installed in 1753. (PH.)

Sunlight streams into the attic space of Independence Hall, revealing the many trusses that support the roof. Several of these large timbers date to the construction of the building in the 1730s. To prevent the floors below from sagging, they are connected to steel hangers and are attached to the trusses. The trusses are numbered, as seen in this 1929 image. (PH.)

The tower clock mechanism, shown concealed in this room in 1929, operates the four clock faces on the tower of Independence Hall. The original clock mechanism installed in 1828 was manufactured by Lukens Clock Factory of Philadelphia. In preparation for the Centennial Exhibition in 1876, Philadelphia resident Henry Seybert donated to the city a new clock and bell to be placed in the tower of Independence Hall. (PH.)

The clock mechanism that Henry Seybert donated has continued to function and toll the hour since 1876. The giant timepiece, seen here in 2008, was manufactured by the Seth Thomas Clock Company in Thomaston, Connecticut. The clock is a gravity escapement and weighs 6,000 pounds. The cast iron frame is 10 feet long and 8 feet high; the pendulum weighs nearly 750 pounds and takes two seconds to swing in one direction. (CA.)

In 1915, electric arc lights and reflectors were installed behind the four clock faces in the tower. A series of bulbs were installed by William A. Heine. This image shows the reflector material set behind each bulb to disperse the light through the clock faces. By 1929, the arc bulbs were replaced by incandescent fixtures that were attached to the walls. Each face was lit by six bulbs. (FLP.)

A rare view behind the clock faces of Independence Hall is seen here in 1929. At the center of the room stands the mechanism that operates the hands of the clock controlled by the Seth Thomas timepiece, located one level below. The clock faces are made of flashed glass, with a white-glass exterior. The approximate diameter of the clock faces are nine feet, four inches; the numerals range from 16 to 19 inches tall. (PH.)

The Palladian window of Independence Hall from the Tower Room stairway in 1959 is one of the distinct trademarks of the building. Typical of European architecture, Palladian windows were mostly incorporated in structures that represented a form of stature, wealth, and high social standing. The portraits that appear on the landing are Lafayette by Thomas Sully (left) and Conrad Alexandre Gerard by Charles Willson Peale (right). (LC.)

The interior of Independence Hall contains beautiful, handcrafted ornamentation and scroll work. An example is this carved face on an open-scrolled pediment over the central hall north door. In 1917, Philadelphia mayor Thomas B. Smith requested a detailed documentation of the architecture of the Independence Hall Complex. His concern was that if the structures were to be destroyed either by nature or man the buildings could be reconstructed. (LC.)

A structural survey was conducted by the George M. Ewing Company in the early 1960s. Their report suggested that steel supports be installed in Independence Hall. After much debate, it was agreed that the installation of the steel would not jeopardize the historic integrity of the structure. This December 1962 image shows a steel girder being hoisted through one of the second-floor windows. (INHP.)

The renovation project of Independence Hall was a major undertaking. Many of the old load-bearing supports were replaced with steel reinforcements. By November 1964, one of the major support beams was in place on the second floor. This beam now divides the Long Room and the Committee of the Assembly Chamber. Morris Wheeler and Company, Inc., formerly of Philadelphia, was the manufacturer of this girder. (INHP.)

The refurbishing of Independence Hall fell under the Mission 66 program. This project was a nationwide effort by the National Park Service to "dramatically expand Park Service visitor services by 1966." Shown here in August 1962, some crew members of the Mission 66 are, from left to right, Casey Gillard, John Egion, John Pecoraio, Roland Verfaillie, Edward Giordano, Fred Suinonser, Leotha Wise, and Edmund Whitlock. (INHP.)

A group of schoolchildren listen to a National Park Service guide in the Assembly Room on November 4, 1964, while renovations are under way. Whenever a construction project is undertaken at Independence Hall, every effort is made to continue to make the structure accessible to visitors. This is evident with the workman in the background attaching a mock ceiling panel and molding of the original to the ceiling. (INHP.)

Three

INDEPENDENCE HALL COMPLEX

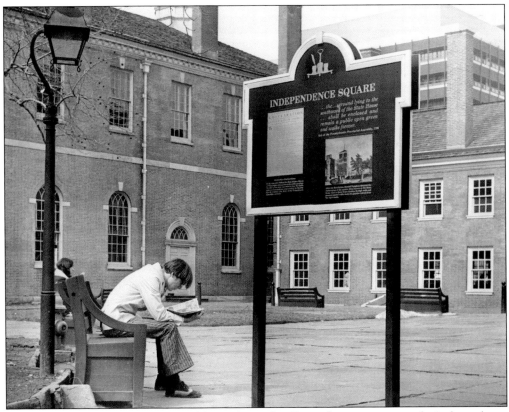

Independence Square is a five-acre public garden and walkway that encompasses the Independence Hall Complex. A 1736 law asserted that the Pennsylvania State House Yard was "to remain a public open green and walks forever," as seen in this 1972 photograph. English landscaper Samuel Vaughan Jr. developed the square into a relaxing sanctuary of foliage and walkways around 1785. The design of the square has changed over time, but its purpose has remained. (UA.)

A view of Independence Square in 1929, facing the northwest, shows two earlier city skyscrapers—the Curtis Building (left) and Public Ledger Building (right)—shadowing the square. Independence Hall can be seen in the center surrounded by the other structures that make up the Independence Square complex: Congress Hall, Old City Hall (both east and west wings), and the American Philosophical Society. (INHP.)

This 1929 view of Independence Square was taken from atop the tower of Independence Hall. The walkways through the square were designed by commissioner of Markets and City Property William Dixey and were installed in 1875 in anticipation of the nation's centennial celebration. Noticeable in the picture are, from left to right, the Temperance Fountain along the left-hand walkway, the Commodore Barry statue, and the Curtis Building. (INHP.)

William Birch captures the elegance of the Walnut Street entrance to Independence Square in this 1800 lithograph. A large, door-like gate opened onto Independence Square, allowing the public to stroll along a series of gravel walkways. In 1812, the seven-foot wall that surrounded the square was lowered to three feet to improve air circulation. Visible is a portion of the Walnut Street prison, seen on the far left. (CA.)

Independence Square has not always been as well-maintained as it is today. In this c. 1867 view, a wrought iron gate with an ornate design and fence surrounds the square. However, missing lamps upon the gate posts suggest an apparent neglect of Independence Square. Dealing with vagrancy and vandalism was also a struggle. Stools were placed throughout the square along the walkways instead of benches to deter loitering. (CA.)

The statue of Commodore John Barry, seen in this c. 1908 photograph in Independence Square, was designed by Samuel Murray and dedicated on March 16, 1907, by the Friendly Sons of St. Patrick. Barry, an Irish-American Revolutionary War commander, is recognized as both the first American-commissioned naval officer and its first flag officer. A regular tradition of wreath laying was instituted by sailors at the Barry statue every Memorial Day. (LC.)

This is a c. 1880 image of the Washington statue in front of Independence Hall. It was created by J.A. Bailly and presented to the city by the First School District of Pennsylvania on July 4, 1869. In 1888, the marble surface of the statue was damaged after being washed with muriatic acid. It was moved to the second floor of Philadelphia City Hall in 1910. The present bronze statue is molded from the Bailly statue. (CA.)

In preparation for the Centennial Exhibition of 1876, held in Philadelphia, new walkways and landscaping were installed around Independence Hall and the square. Seen here c. 1875, large flagstone slabs lean against Independence Hall awaiting installation as part of the preparation for this six month-long event. In 1974, this flagstone walkway was removed in preparation for the nation's bicentennial. (CA.)

Independence Square underwent a large-scale renovation project beginning in 1915. This was largely inspired by the American Institute of Architects. In this March 1915 image, workmen can be seen raising the retaining wall surrounding the square using molded brick on the northeast corner of Sixth and Walnut Streets. Horace Sellers, the architect, recommended the walls around the square be built "in detail strictly in accord with the practice in the 18th century." (PH.)

In 2004, a full-scale renovation project of Independence Square was begun. Work of this magnitude had not been done since 1916. The project included the replacement of broken flagstones within the walkway of the square, which were laid prior to the 1876 Centennial Exposition. Dan Lepore and Sons Company of Conshohocken, Pennsylvania, were able to combine a mixture of new flagstone and former pieces to complete the project. (CA.)

During the Independence Square restoration in 2004, digging required close attention. Concern with disrupting archaeological remains was given high priority. Due to the use of heavy machinery, a team of trained archaeologists were on hand to observe any disruption of archaeological remains or discovery of historic objects. Employees of the JPC Group are shown installing a geotextile fabric, which allows drainage beneath the flagstone walkways. (CA.)

Another portion of the restoration of Independence Square was the replacement of the drainage system. Many of the former ceramic pipes, which dated back to the 1860s, had either cracked or collapsed, hindering proper flow of drainage water from the square. The JPC Group of Blackwood, New Jersey, was contracted to install the new drainage system. (CA.)

Throughout the reconstruction of the square, Independence Hall continued to remain open to the public. Fencing and pathways safely directed visitors through the square and into the buildings. Each day brought new challenges for both construction crews and National Park Service staff alike. The project was completed in the fall of 2005 with fully restored walkways, drainage systems, and lighting. Some archaeological findings were discovered and recorded for further study. (CA.)

During the restoration of Independence Square, 56 lamps were installed, each representing a signer of the Declaration of Independence. They were designed to be lit either by electricity or gas. In the 1950s, the lamps were changed to operate primarily by electricity. Shown here in this 1956 photograph, a maintenance man is seen replacing one of the bulbs. As of this date, some of the lamps have been removed. (INHP.)

In 1876, a public fountain was installed in Independence Square by the Sons of Temperance Grand Division of Pennsylvania. Seen here in 1953, the fountain was deemed unhygienic in 1961 by the United States Health Service. They recommended that the fountain be removed. New modern bubbler heads were installed that year in response, but the new sanitary bubbler heads were ultimately a failure, and the fountain was removed in 1968. (UA.)

The District Court House, shown here c. 1898, was built by the City of Philadelphia in 1867. Located on Sixth Street behind Congress Hall (far left), the structure also housed the library for the University of Pennsylvania's Law School. The building was demolished in 1901 as part of a plan to restore the Independence Hall Complex to its appearance during the Colonial era. (INHP.)

This c. 1950 view shows a driveway leading into the plaza behind Independence Hall, which was created after the demolition of the District Court House in 1901. Two Civil War cannons were installed at the top of the driveway in 1919. The general purpose of the driveway is to allow vehicles to enter the square to maintain the structures and landscaping within the Independence Hall Complex and prepare for events. (INHP.)

On December 24, 1913, over 20,000 spectators filled Independence Square to watch the lighting of an 80-foot spruce Christmas tree. Lueretia Blankenburg, wife of Philadelphia mayor Rudolph Blankenburg, threw the switch to light the star that contained 56 little stars representing each of the signers of the Declaration of Independence. Mayor Blankenburg had the honor of lighting the tree, which was decorated with 4,200 red, white, and blue lights. (INHP.)

During a visit to Philadelphia on September 12, 1919, Gen. John J. Pershing visited Independence Hall. After a tour of the building, the general was escorted into Independence Square where he was given the honor of planting a tree. Using a brand-new brass shovel, he was heard saying when he finished, "May you live long and prosper." It is believed that this tree no longer stands. (INHP.)

The northeast corner of Independence Square is seen here as it appeared in 1939. Taken by photographer Frederick D. Nichols for the Historic American Buildings Survey, the photograph shows several of the main structures surrounding the square. From left to right are Independence Hall, the East Wing, Old City Hall, and the American Philosophical Society. (LC.)

Visitors gather in Independence Square on July 8, 1979, as a Colonial-dressed interpreter reenacts the first public reading of the Declaration of Independence. It was on this date in 1776 that the document with which the American colonies declared independence from Britain was first read publicly. The reading took place upon a platform constructed as part of an observatory for the Transit of Venus in 1769. (INHP.)

Congress Hall, located on the southeast corner of Sixth and Chestnut Streets, was the home of the United States Congress from 1790 to 1800. Originally constructed to house the government offices of Philadelphia County, congress held its first session here on December 6, 1790. This 1900 image was taken on the last day the building was occupied by the Law Department of the University of Pennsylvania. (INHP.)

In 1800, the federal government moved from Philadelphia and relocated to the established federal city of Washington. Congress Hall was then returned to its original use as the Philadelphia County Courthouse. In 1870, the Pennsylvania Assembly ordered buildings surrounding Independence Hall to be demolished. The orders were repealed in 1895. The structure soon underwent much-needed restoration. In 1913, work was completed and the building rededicated by Pres. Woodrow Wilson. (PH.)

The House of Representatives Chamber in Congress Hall is seen here as it appeared c. 1898. The room was utilized as a courtroom for the City of Philadelphia. In 1897, the room served as a lecture hall for law students attending the Law School of the University of Pennsylvania. In February 1900, the Law Department vacated Congress Hall, as a new building was opened on the main Penn campus for the department. (INHP.)

This room, once located on the second floor of Congress Hall, was used as a lecture room for the third-year class attending the Law School of the University of Pennsylvania c. 1898. The room was constructed as the Supreme Court Room. In 1912, the American Institute of Architects restored the interior of Congress Hall to what it believed to be the original appearance of the building. (INHP.)

In this 1918 photograph, the artwork of Philadelphia-born artist Jean Leon Gerome Ferris was displayed in the House of Representatives Chamber in Congress Hall. The exhibit titled the *Pageant of a Nation* contained 60 paintings depicting various events in American history. Ferris trained professionally at the Pennsylvania Academy of Fine Arts. Together, these pieces of artwork were the largest series of American historical paintings executed by a single artist. (PH.)

Shown here is the House of Representatives Chamber in Congress Hall c. 1930. The exhibition gallery had been removed, and a study was being conducted at this time to add furniture that best fit the period in which the United States Congress occupied the room. Many historic events occurred here: the ratification of the Bill of Rights, the second inauguration of George Washington, and the inauguration of John Adams. (CA.)

A merchant sells produce on the southeast corner of Sixth and Chestnut Streets in 1913. Noticeable is the stairway leading to the front entrance of Congress Hall. Today, this area is cordoned off, and pedestrians are restricted to the opposite side of Chestnut Street, except by entering through security. This photograph illustrates how the Independence Hall Complex was very much a part of the daily routine of the citizens of the city. (PH.)

Shown in this c. 1880 photograph is Independence Hall and accompanying buildings looking southwest on Chestnut Street. All city government offices were located here before relocating to the present city hall. Visible from left to right are Old City Hall, the east wing occupied by the clerk of the Mayor's Court, recorder of deeds and wills, Independence Hall, where city council met, the west wing occupied by the sheriff's office, and Congress Hall. (CA.)

Old City Hall, seen c. 1920 on the southwest corner of Fifth and Chestnut Streets, is part of the Independence Square Complex. Construction began in the summer of 1790. Although built for city use, it served as the home of the first Supreme Court of the United States from 1791 to 1800. When the federal government moved to Washington, Old City Hall returned to its intended use as a place for city government. (CA.)

Looking east on Chestnut Street, Old City Hall in 1913 stands dilapidated and vacant. By the mid-1890s, Old City Hall was abandoned. All city government offices had relocated to the new Philadelphia City Hall at Penn Square. This picture reveals the scarring of a former two-story brick addition that once was attached to the west wall of the building. In 1921, restoration began on the structure, and it was rededicated on May 2, 1922. (PH.)

The entry hall of Old City Hall is seen as it appeared in 1923. The American Institute of Architects remodeled the interior as closely as possible to its original appearance. Renovations were initially to begin c. 1917, but the onset of World War I caused the project to be delayed. The building served as a museum that included historic artifacts and paintings when it was rededicated in 1922. (INHP.)

The Mayor's Court room in Old City Hall in 1927 was utilized as a museum. Flags of Colonial America adorn the spectator's gallery while historic artifacts and furnishings are exhibited below. During Constitution Week in September 2011, a historic event occurred in the former Mayor's Court. The Pennsylvania Supreme Court, the nation's oldest appellate court, convened in the historic space for the first time in more than two centuries. (INHP.)

With the onset of the Great Depression, vagrancy and crime became an issue around the Independence Hall Complex. City officers patrolled the perimeter of the square. Officers Coull, Watson, Murhill, and Schwartz stand at attention on April 24, 1929, between the structures of Old City Hall to the left and the north wall of the American Philosophical Society to the right. (PH.)

The American Philosophical Society was founded by Benjamin Franklin in 1743. The society was established to promote the pursuit of "useful knowledge." Philosophical Hall, shown here in 1917, is the only privately owned structure on Independence Square. Constructed in 1789, a third-floor addition was added as a library in 1891 and removed in 1949. The library was relocated to a newly constructed facility across the street. (PH.)

Four

THE LIBERTY BELL

For nearly two centuries, the Liberty Bell has remained silent, no longer tolling the majestic tone it was intended to produce. But has it really kept silent? The inscription encircling the bell's crown has spoken volumes to so many: "Proclaim Liberty thro' all the Land to all the inhabitants thereof Leviticus 25:10." The Liberty Bell is not only a symbol of freedom for Americans, but for many around the world. (LC.)

In November 1751, the Pennsylvania Assembly sent word to London that they wanted to "procure a bell" to hang in the state house steeple. Isaac Norris sent instructions to Robert Charles to "get us a good bell, of about two thousand pounds weight, the cost of which, we presume may amount to about one hundred pounds sterling." The bell was cast by the Whitechapel Bell Foundry in London in 1752. (CA.)

The bell arrived in Philadelphia in September 1752. Isaac Norris notes, "The bell is come on shore and in good order." When tested "cracked by a stroke of the clapper." It was agreed to send the bell back to London, but the ship returning could not take it aboard. The bell was melted down and recast twice by Philadelphia founders Pass and Stow in order to create the present bell. (CA.)

In September 1777, the British Army overpowered Gen. George Washington's troops at Brandywine Creek, leaving Philadelphia vulnerable for attack. The Pennsylvania Supreme Executive Council ordered that all bells be removed from the city, fearing the British would melt them down and recast them into cannons to be used against Colonial troops. The Liberty Bell, depicted in this 1940s Philadelphia Whiskey advertisement, was hidden in Allentown, Pennsylvania. (FLP.)

In 1872, the original framework that once supported the Liberty Bell was brought down from the belfry. The bell was reattached and displayed beneath the stairway of the Tower Room. Secretary of the Navy George M. Robeson approved the loan of his men to lower the framework from the tower. The work was accomplished on January 13, 1873. (CA.)

VESTIBULE, INDEPENDENCE HALL.

In 1876, visitors were able to admire the Liberty Bell located on the floor level of the Tower Room. The bell was placed behind a gated structure beneath the staircase leading to the second floor of Independence Hall. Prior to the centennial, many felt that the bell's crack should be repaired. The Philadelphia City Council and the Committee on Restoration of Independence Hall voted against the plan. (INHP.)

On March 20, 1877, the Philadelphia Common Council passed a resolution to suspend the Liberty Bell from the ceiling of the Tower Room in Independence Hall. The chain contained 13 links, each representing one of the 13 original colonies. The bell remained suspended in the Tower Room until 1885, when it was taken down to be exhibited at the World's Industrial and Cotton Centennial Exhibition in New Orleans. (FLP.)

A Philadelphia police officer leans against the wooden supports that once held the Liberty Bell in the tower of Independence Hall. When the bell was hung from the Tower Room ceiling in 1877, the supports were placed in Independence Square. Through public outcry to preserve them, they were offered to the Pennsylvania Historical Society. They declined, and the timbers were stored in the tower where they remain today. (INHP.)

When the Liberty Bell returned from the 1893 Chicago World's Columbian Exposition, it was placed in a glass case designed by Francis D. Kramer. Rollers were constructed on the bottom of the case in order to swiftly remove the bell from Independence Hall in case of emergency. If the bell continued to hang from the ceiling of the Tower Room, it would be impossible to remove quickly. (INHP.)

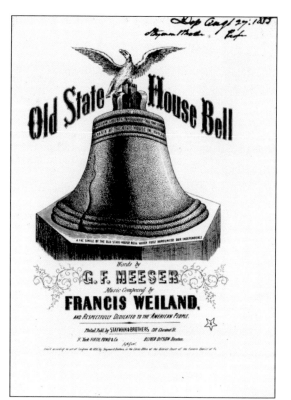

The Liberty Bell has been honored in song since the mid-1800s. These songs draw on patriotic emotions that the Liberty Bell conveys. The "Old State House Bell" is possibly the earliest known piece of music honoring the Liberty Bell. It was composed in 1855 by Francis Weiland with lyrics by George F. Meeser, both Philadelphians. The composition was "Respectfully Dedicated to the American People." (DU.)

"The Liberty Bell" is one of the most recognized and popular pieces of music written to pay tribute to the historic relic. In 1893, American composer and conductor John Philip Sousa was inspired by a display of the Liberty Bell at the Columbian Exposition in Chicago to title a pre-composed march to honor the bell. The United States Marine Corps Band has played the march for three presidential inaugurations. (LC.)

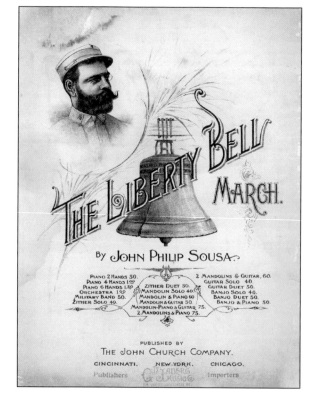

"Liberty Bell (It's Time to Ring Again)" was written in 1917 by composer Halsey K. Mohr and lyricist Joe Goodwin. Pres. Woodrow Wilson advocated noninvolvement as the nation approached the beginning of World War I. The lyrics call for Americans to become involved in defeating the enemy by using the Liberty Bell as inspiration. "It's time to wake 'em up, It's time to shake 'em up, It's a cause worth ringing for." (LC.)

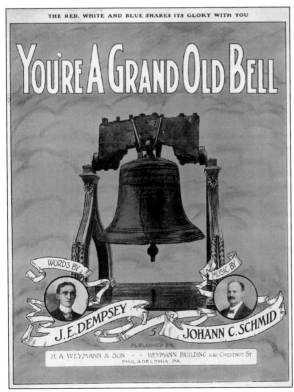

"You're A Grand Old Bell," composed in 1919, was another patriotic song written to honor the Liberty Bell. J.E. Dempsey wrote the lyrics, and the music was composed by Johann C. Schmid, a native of Philadelphia. The song is cast in an upbeat, march-like form and honors the bell with the words: "Dear old emblem, your voice proclaimed that our land was, at last a free one." (LC.)

65

Hidden beneath the Liberty Bell is an interesting piece of framework. Devised by J. Sellers Bancroft, the metal structure placed inside the bell is called the "spider." Its purpose is to hold the bell's weight to prevent any further cracking. The spider was attached in May 1915 in preparation for the bell's long westward journey to San Francisco. Many felt that the long trip would be detrimental to its safety. (CA.)

Chief of city property Harry T. Baxter holds the Liberty Bell steady while engineer Fred Eckerseng (standing left) and an unidentified man fasten reinforcing plates on the yoke of the bell in 1929. The yoke is made from American elm, also known as slippery elm, and is believe to be the original wood. The yoke weighs 200 pounds; this is about one-tenth the weight of the Liberty Bell itself. (INHP.)

Chief of city property of Philadelphia Harry T. Baxter sits before the Liberty Bell in this *Pacific & Atlantic Photo* on New Year's Eve 1923. At 11:45 p.m., he broadcast live the history of the bell. At the stroke of midnight, the bell was tapped to symbolically ring in the New Year. The broadcast was aired across the United States, and a special effort was made to reach foreign nations. (CA.)

Descendants of Andrew McNair gather around the Liberty Bell on November 1, 1951, for its 200th anniversary. Legend is told that McNair raced up the tower stairs of the Pennsylvania State House to ring the bell announcing the signing of the Declaration of Independence on July 4, 1776. Actor William Duell portrayed McNair in the play and movie *1776*. (INHP.)

Guards at Independence Hall practice removing the Liberty Bell to a secure location in the event that Philadelphia fell under attack. Shortly after the United States entered World War II on December 7, 1941, the country was on high alert. Measures were taken to protect the Liberty Bell in the event that Philadelphia was bombed. This 1942 image shows the bell on wheels to be easily rolled to safety. (UA.)

In the event of a military attack on Philadelphia during World War II, a bomb-proof vault to protect the Liberty Bell was considered. This diagram illustrates the vault beneath the floor of the Tower Room. The bell would be lowered into the encasement and safe from harm. Despite an offer from the Insurance Company of North America for the construction of the vault, the project never went into effect. (UA.)

In 1962, the National Park Service invited the Franklin Institute of Philadelphia to conduct a study of the Liberty Bell and the wood yoke that bears the bell's weight. In response, the Committee for the Preservation of the Liberty Bell was established. It was hoped that the research would reveal the crack's extent and how to prevent further cracking in the future and whether the wood yoke needed replacing or strengthening. (INHP.)

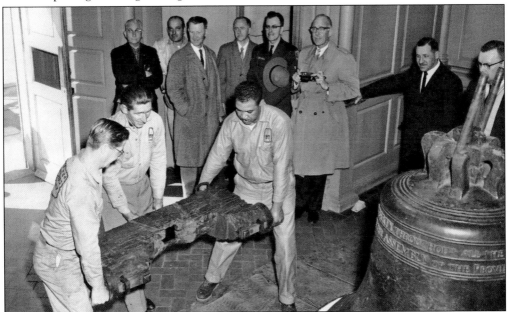

The yoke of the Liberty Bell is being reattached after a series of tests and refurbishing was completed in 1962 by the Franklin Institute. The studies revealed that the spider attached to the bell in 1915 was highly successful in stopping the spread of the crack. The study also revealed the metal mixtures of the bell were beginning to age, causing a very gradual weakening of the bell's metal. (INHP.)

The how, when, and why the Liberty Bell received its famous crack has been a mystery and debate for generations. It was first reported that the bell cracked during a visit by the Marquis de Lafayette in 1824. Another claim is the bell cracked while ringing to celebrate George Washington's birthday on February 22, 1832. One of the most commonly cited dates is July 8, 1835, when the bell rang for the funeral of Chief Justice John Marshall. William Eckel, superintendent of the old Pennsylvania State House, ordered that the crack be drilled out in 1846, giving the bell its famous trademark. This was to prevent the edges from vibrating when the bell rang. In the latter part of the 19th century, the Liberty Bell traveled extensively by rail, being jarred and jostled along the way. It was soon discovered the crack spread further into the crown. Scientific analyses have shown that the metal content in the bell shows a higher content of softer metals than harder ones. Overall the bell still remains for all to see. (INHP.)

In 1975, the Eastman Kodak Company was commissioned by the Independence National Historical Park to create a radiograph of the Liberty Bell. This process, similar to an X-ray, was to determine whether the bell could handle the move to a new location across the street from Independence Hall. In preparation for the nation's bicentennial celebration, a new home was constructed for the Liberty Bell to handle the flow of visitors. (CA.)

The radiograph test conducted in 1975 on the Liberty Bell by the Eastman Kodak Company took two consecutive nights in October and a third in November. The test revealed that the bell contains several small cracks. It was determined, however, that it could handle the move to the new pavilion without further concern of cracking. (CA.)

Ground breaking for the Liberty Bell Pavilion was held on March 5, 1975. Mayor Frank L. Rizzo (right) and other officials break ground for the construction of the $836,000 glass and steel structure that would house the Liberty Bell in Independence Mall. The Mitchell/Giurgola Associates, architects of the pavilion, designed the structure to allow the Liberty Bell and Independence Hall to be viewed together from Market Street. (INHP.)

Construction on the Liberty Bell Pavilion progressed through the fall of 1975. The new exhibit space for the Liberty Bell was to allow the flow of visitors to see the historic relic during the highly anticipated bicentennial celebration. The Philadelphia-based company J.J. White, Inc., constructed the pavilion, which would accommodate more visitors than the space in the Tower Room of Independence Hall. (UA.)

The interior of the Liberty Bell Pavilion was under construction in 1975. Behind the scaffolding, the new stand upon which the Liberty Bell would rest is set in place. The pavilion also contained a taped commentary on the history of the bell in several different languages. The bell would be displayed facing Market Street with Independence Hall visible in the background. (UA.)

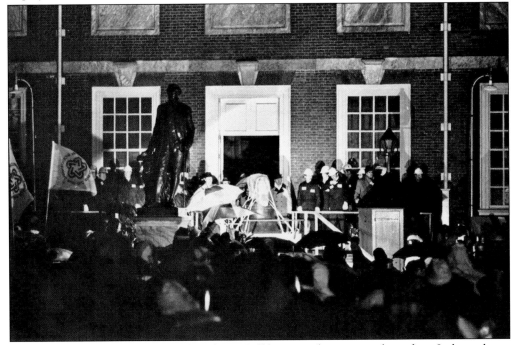

At 12:01 a.m. on January 1, 1976, the Liberty Bell began its long-awaited trip from Independence Hall to its new home in the pavilion. The bell, seen covered with plastic to help protect it from a soaking rain, took less than 25 minutes to travel the 100 yards to its new home. A special ramp was constructed to aid the descent of the bell onto Chestnut Street. (INHP.)

Despite the rain, thousands braved the weather to see the historic move. It was reported that the crowds along the pathway were five to six lines deep. Flashbulbs popped as the 2,080-pound Liberty Bell was led to its new location. Once inside the pavilion, it took several minutes for the bell to be lowered into place. It was estimated that it cost the city $104,000 to move the bell. (INHP.)

This is the picture the architect had envisioned—the Liberty Bell in a new modern space with Independence Hall as a backdrop. It was soon discovered sunlight streaming from the skylight above caused the bell to heat, thus expanding and contracting frequently. This placed much stress on the bell and its crack. Also, it was discovered that exhaust fumes from traffic on Market Street caused oxidation within the bell's interior surface. (LC.)

Despite controversy over the design of the structure, the opening of the Liberty Bell Pavilion was a great success. The National Park Service reported a record 50,800 visitors the weekend of Washington's birthday in 1976. In 2003, the pavilion would be removed to unblock the view from Independence Hall to the National Constitution Center two blocks north. The pavilion was dismantled and shipped to Anchorage, Alaska. (INHP.)

On October 9, 2003, the Liberty Bell moved into a new $12.9-million exhibition facility. The new Liberty Bell Center offers visitors a more museum-like atmosphere. The center contains Liberty Bell artifacts and image-filled wall panels to interpret the history of the bell. This photograph shows Independence Mall looking north in 2003. From left to right are the Liberty Bell Center, Independence Visitors Center, National Constitution Center, and Liberty Bell Pavilion. (LC.)

The Centennial Bell, which hangs in the belfry of Independence Hall, was cast in 1876. As the Liberty Bell could no longer be rung properly, a new bell was cast by the Meneely and Kimberly Bell Foundry of Troy, New York. The Centennial Bell weighs 13,000 pounds, representing each of the 13 original colonies, and its metals are from four cannons, one from each side in the American Revolution and the Civil War. (INHP.)

Consul General Denis E. Richards of Britain (left) and Supt. Hobart C. Cawood of Independence National Historical Park admire the new Bicentennial Bell given as a gift from Britain to the United States in July 1976. The bell was hoisted up the 123-foot tower of the Independence National Historical Park Visitor Center at Third and Chestnut Streets. The bell was cast by the Whitechapel Foundry, the same that cast the first Pennsylvania State House Bell in 1752. (INHP.)

Five

THE LIBERTY BELL'S TRAVELS PROMOTE PATRIOTISM

Americans in the late 19th century began to revere the Liberty Bell as a symbol of their independence and liberty. Philadelphia officials began receiving requests for the historic symbol to be exhibited in their state. For the first time, the Liberty Bell left Independence Hall and toured the nation, from 1885 to 1915. Shown is the Liberty Bell on a float during the 225th anniversary parade of the founding of Philadelphia in 1908. (PH.)

The Liberty Bell is seen displayed on a flatcar to be exhibited at the World's Industrial and Cotton Centennial Exposition in New Orleans in 1885. Special commissioner for the exhibition S. Prentiss Nutt petitioned the mayor of Philadelphia, William B. Smith, in 1884 to send the bell to New Orleans, claiming that it would be met "with the universal approbation and the heartiest greetings of all the people of the South." (KS.)

The Liberty Bell left Philadelphia on January 23, 1885, guarded by 48 police officers, 3 of whom are shown here. The bell arrived in New Orleans three days later. It was reported that the exposition was successful but not without controversy. A New Orleans taxpayer sued the city over the cost for returning the bell to Philadelphia. Unfortunately, the City of Philadelphia had to absorb the cost of the bell's return. (KS.)

On June 13, 1885, the Liberty Bell left New Orleans on the Louisville & Nashville Railroad and made its way northward. Before reaching Philadelphia, the bell stopped in Montgomery, Alabama; Richmond, Virginia; and Baltimore, Maryland. It was in Baltimore where a delegation from Philadelphia joined the mayor of New Orleans and traveled together on the last leg of the trip to Philadelphia. The Liberty Bell arrived in Philadelphia on June 17 amid a grand reception. After removing the bell from the train at Germantown Junction, it was escorted to Broad and Diamond Streets, where the parade began. The parade then proceeded towards Independence Hall. Residents along the parade route decorated their homes with flags and bunting. This one-sided flier presumably was circulated throughout Philadelphia welcoming the Liberty Bell home. It contains a poem written by author Edward J. Virtue. The first part of the poem reads, "Welcome! welcome back, belov'd Old Liberty Bell. Thy voice when young on three million Enthrall'd souls fell; Heralding their bold Declaration to all lands, Of their Independence from a cruel tyrant's hands." (CA.)

In 1893, the Liberty Bell traveled to Chicago, Illinois, to be exhibited at the Columbian Exposition. Pres. Grover Cleveland was among the spectators who welcomed the bell. Crowds lined the route as the Liberty Bell was transported to its temporary home in a replica of Independence Hall. Concerns quickly surfaced when the present crack was seen to be expanding upward into the bell's crown. (FLP.)

Shown in this 1893 photograph, taken at the closing of the Columbian Exposition, Philadelphians rally around the Liberty Bell, at right. Pictured on the left is the Troy Bell, made for the Daughters of the American Revolution at the Charles H. Meneely Bell Company of Troy, New York. The bell was made of metallic historic artifacts donated from all over the country, including a link from Pres. Abraham Lincoln's gold watch chain. (CA.)

In 1895, the Liberty Bell traveled to Atlanta, Georgia, to be exhibited at the Cotton States and International Exposition. The bell left Philadelphia and made frequent stops along the way to cheering crowds, speeches, and great fanfare. The fair took place at Atlanta's Piedmont Park amid throngs of nearly 800,000 visitors who attended the three-month exposition. The bell can be seen displayed to the right under a striped canopy. (AHC.)

The Cotton States and International Exposition attracted visitors from the United States and 13 countries. The exposition is most remembered for a speech that was given by African American civil rights leader Booker T. Washington. A specially designed rubber cushion was made to prevent further cracking of the bell as it traveled by rail. The bell can be seen resting on its new support frame as children pose for a photograph. (AHC.)

On January 6, 1902, the Liberty Bell was removed from Independence Hall once again and loaded onto a horse-drawn wagon in preparation to appear at the Carolina Interstate and West Indian Exposition in Charleston, South Carolina. Despite controversy surrounding the travels of the Liberty Bell, there was great optimism that sending the bell to South Carolina would strengthen unity between the northern and southern states. (INHP.)

Amid ceremony and fanfare on Chestnut Street, the Liberty Bell rests upon a decorated float drawn by four horses. The float was covered with American flags; red, white, and blue bunting; flowers; and various patriotic symbols. Guarded by Philadelphia police officers, the bell was taken to the Pennsylvania Railroad. Hundreds of spectators lined the bell's route to the rail yard where it would begin the three-day journey to Charleston. (INHP.)

Spectators flock to the freight yard as the Liberty Bell is hoisted by a derrick from the decorative float and loaded upon a flatcar, seen on the right. Here, it was mounted onto a display stand and stabilized to prevent any rocking while traveling. As the train pulled from the station, a 21-gun salute was fired from League Island along the Delaware River, by order of the secretary of the Navy. (INHP.)

As a patriotic gesture, the Liberty Bell made numerous stops along the way to Charleston. The route selected for the trip included stops in Pennsylvania, Maryland, Virginia, West Virginia, Tennessee, North Carolina, South Carolina, and Georgia. All along the route, adults and children enjoyed posing with the bell for a photographic souvenir. (INHP.)

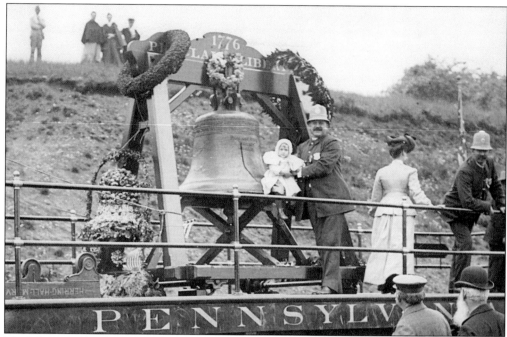

The Liberty Bell makes a stop in Plainfield, Connecticut, on June 16, 1903, as it traveled to Boston, Massachusetts, to celebrate the 128th anniversary of the Battle of Bunker Hill. A request was made several years earlier by Boston for the celebration of the battle's 125th anniversary but was denied by Philadelphia City Council. In March 1903, Mayor Patrick Collins of Boston made the plea again; this time it was granted. (INHP.)

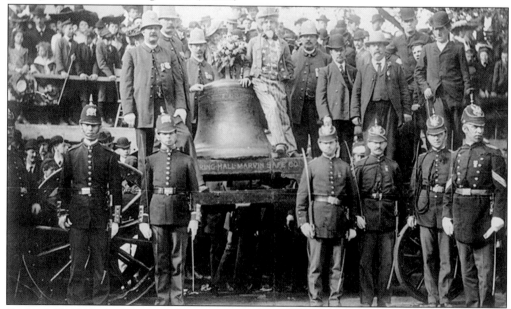

On June 17, 1903, the Liberty Bell was loaded upon a wagon drawn by a team of 13 horses, each horse representing one of the original colonies. An excerpt from the *Philadelphia Inquirer* reads, "Sam Daniel O'Riorden, of Charlestown, dressed as Uncle Sam gathered up the reins, and the bell began its journey to the shrine of Bunker Hill." O'Riorden is seen standing to the right of the bell. (LC.)

As the Liberty Bell made its way to Charlestown, the site of Bunker Hill, the bell was received with great cheers, hand clapping, and waving of flags by thousands who came to see it. A newspaper account reported that "For nearly two hours the crowds kept coming and going, taking a look at the famous old relic. Many insisted on placing their hands on it." (CA.)

Photographer Thomas E. Marr captures members of the Ancient and Honorable Artillery Company of Massachusetts standing proudly next to the Liberty Bell, for the celebration of the 128th anniversary of the Battle of Bunker Hill. The Ancients escorted the bell in the afternoon parade that was commanded by Col. Sidney M. Hedges. Colonel Hedges is presumably the gentleman standing to the far right. (CA.)

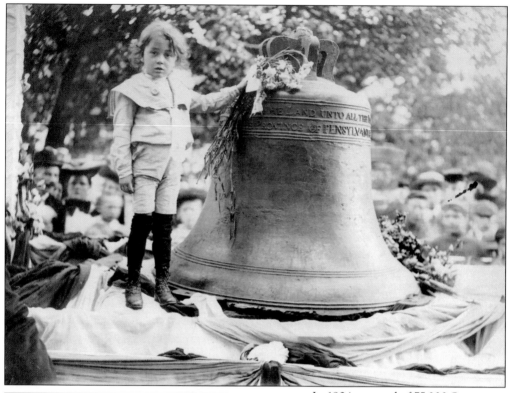

In 1904, a crowd of 75,000 St. Louis schoolchildren successfully petitioned the Pennsylvania Commission to have the Liberty Bell exhibited at the Louisiana Purchase Exposition in St. Louis, Missouri. The fair was located on the grounds of present-day Forest Park and on the campus of Washington University. The fair contained over 1,500 buildings. As shown here, children were often closely associated with the Liberty Bell. (MSHS.)

The Liberty Bell arrived in St. Louis on June 8, 1904, and was greeted with a traditional setting of patriotic bunting, American flags, wreaths, and bell facsimiles. The Liberty Bell traveled through eight states on its five-day journey to St. Louis. The trip would take the bell as far north as Minnesota. Philadelphia mayor John Weaver accompanied the bell on this trip, in addition to a police escort. (MHM.)

On December 9, 1912, Emma Doane presents Mayor Rudolph Blankenburg of Philadelphia with a petition signed by 500,000 children of California requesting the Liberty Bell be sent to San Francisco to be exhibited during the Panama-Pacific International Exhibition in 1915. The petition was carried on a reel measuring more than 10 feet in diameter. Doane was chosen to represent the children as a result of a newspaper popularity contest. (INHP.)

On the afternoon of June 5, 1915, the Liberty Bell was paraded along Market Street among throngs of spectators as it made its way to the rail yard to begin the journey west. The parade route was decorated with American flags, adding to the festive atmosphere of the occasion. The building seen in the background is the Lit Brothers Department Store located at Seventh and Market Streets. (INHP.)

Shown here, the Liberty Bell is being hoisted onto a specially designed railroad car on July 5, 1915. Devices on the car included shock absorbers installed to prevent the bell from being jolted or jostled as it traveled. The bell was accompanied by a brigade of the Pennsylvania National Guard. Amid cheers and the usual fanfare, the bell left Philadelphia via the Pennsylvania Railroad. (CA.)

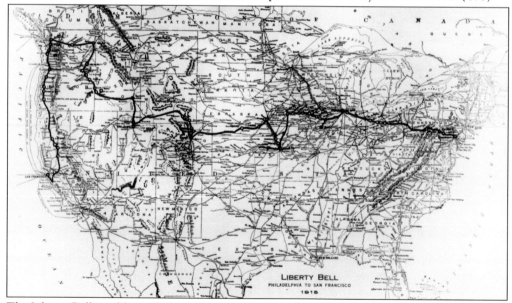

The Liberty Bell would spend almost five months away from Philadelphia. This 1915 map shows the westward route the bell traveled to reach San Francisco. The bell traveled through many of the northern states. On its return trip, the bell took a more southern route. In both directions, the Liberty Bell would stop at various cities and towns to allow Americans the opportunity to see the historic symbol. (INHP.)

As the Liberty Bell passed through America's heartland, it would occasionally stop along the way, allowing many there the opportunity to see this symbol of freedom for the first time. The bell would pass through Missouri, Iowa, Kansas, and Nebraska. On July 8, the bell arrived in Atchison, Kansas, for a five-minute visit. It is evident from this little girl's face that the bell's visit brought much excitement. (INHP.)

On Friday, July 9, the Liberty Bell arrived in Lincoln, Nebraska, for a two-hour stop. Here, this young man, bearing crutches, poses with the bell. Word spread that the Liberty Bell was traveling across the country. At each stop, the crowds grew larger. For many, the opportunity to see, touch, even have a memorable picture taken with the Liberty Bell was something that many cherished for a lifetime. (INHP.)

The Liberty Bell arrived in Denver, Colorado, on July 10, 1915, by way of the Union Pacific Railroad. While there, Denver resident Ethlyn Hembd gently touches the bell as Dr. Clarkson N. Guyer, a dentist originally from Albany, New York, looks on. The bell would stay in Denver for six hours before leaving for LaSalle, Colorado, and then northward to Wyoming. (CA.)

On July 14, 1915, the Liberty Bell makes a historic stop in the community of Auburn, Washington, 20 miles south of Seattle. News of the bell's arrival drew hundreds of spectators. Crowds surrounded the train car to get a closer look, while others climbed upon an adjacent roof top. Dignitaries can be seen aboard the flatcar greeting the crowd; it resembled a political whistle-stop campaign. (CA.)

At 9:30 p.m. on July 16, 1915, the Liberty Bell arrived in San Francisco, California. The following day was proclaimed "Liberty Bell Day." The bell was lowered onto a float decorated with flowers and paraded through the streets of San Francisco. The bell made its way to the fairgrounds and was displayed in the Pennsylvania Building. As a safety precaution during off-hours, the Liberty Bell was secured in a fireproof vault. (INHP.)

The safety of the Liberty Bell was always a top priority during the bell's trip to San Francisco. Four Philadelphia police officers were chosen to protect the bell. Posing just after the Liberty Bell was hoisted onto the float in San Francisco are, from left to right, Joseph Frank, William Sykes, James Quirk, and James Jackson. (INHP.)

The Liberty Bell is displayed atop a beautifully decorated float at the Panama-Pacific International Exposition in 1915 after being paraded through San Francisco. Construction of the exhibition site took over three years to complete. The fair had a great economic impact for San Francisco after nearly being destroyed from an earthquake and fire in 1906. The exhibition was considered a tremendous success and helped to boost morale. (CA.)

The Panama-Pacific International Exposition was a combination celebration. It commemorated the completion of the Panama Canal and also the 400th anniversary of the discovery of the Pacific Ocean. Several cities had applied to host the Panama-Pacific International Exposition. One of the top contenders was New Orleans. After a long competition of advertising and campaigning, Pres. William H. Taft declared San Francisco the official host. (CA.)

American inventor Thomas Alva Edison, most noted for his invention of the electric lightbulb, poses with the Liberty Bell at the Panama-Pacific International Exposition in October 1915. Edison and wife Mina Miller Edison traveled to California to attend events given in his honor at the exposition. Edison may have been most intrigued with how a young General Electric company illuminated the fairgrounds at night with indirect lighting. (INHP.)

Chief Little Bear touches the Liberty Bell at the Panama-Pacific International Exposition in 1915. Little Bear and several members of his tribe were treated to an expense-paid trip to the exhibition to promote the Great Northern Railroad and Glacier National Park. The Liberty Bell may not have represented liberty for these Native Americans, for Glacier National Park was created by land once occupied by Little Bear's people. (INHP.)

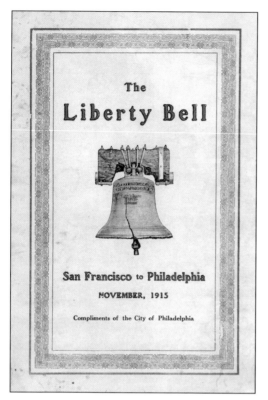

The Liberty Bell

San Francisco to Philadelphia

NOVEMBER, 1915

Compliments of the City of Philadelphia

This 32-page booklet was distributed to visitors along the train route that carried the Liberty Bell back to Philadelphia. The booklet, which was a propaganda push to promote the city of Philadelphia, contained a brief history of the Liberty Bell and the "City of Brotherly Love," along with images of historic sites. A portion also contains a printed version of the Declaration of Independence written by Thomas Jefferson. (CA.)

The Liberty Bell arrives in San Diego to attend the Panama-California Exposition soon after it left San Francisco on November 11, 1915. The bell once again was paraded through the streets before being placed on display. The Liberty Bell remained in San Diego until November 15, when it was placed back on the train and took a 10-day journey through the lower southern states before arriving in Philadelphia. (SDHC.)

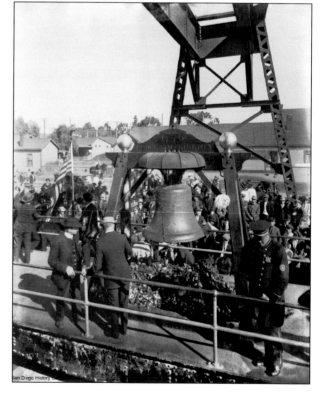

Six

INDEPENDENCE HALL AND THE LIBERTY BELL,

SYMBOLS OF FREEDOM AND INDIVIDUAL RIGHTS

The Fourth of July is the most celebrated patriotic day in the United States, as seen in this 1923 image. John Adams, in a letter to his wife, Abigail, writes, "I am apt to believe that it will be celebrated, by succeeding Generations, as the great anniversary Festival . . . with Pomp and Parade, with Shews [sic], Games, Sports, Bells, Bonfires and Illuminations from one End of this Continent to the other." (LC.)

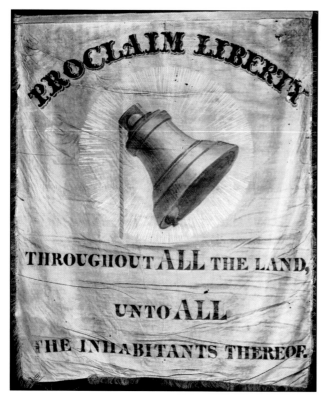

The American Anti-Slavery Society was founded by William Lloyd Garrison in 1833. The society chose the Pennsylvania State House Bell as a symbol for the cause. It was the abolitionists who gave the bell the name "Liberty Bell" from the inscription it bears. This banner, used by Garrison at anti-slavery fairs and festivals throughout Massachusetts, contains a painted image of the bell and "Proclaim Liberty" printed across the top. (MHS.)

The Liberty Bell was a publication by the American Anti-Slavery Society published between 1839 and 1858. The publication featured editorials, poems, and songs written by celebrities of the time. This cover depicts the Liberty Bell hanging from a tree with the words "Proclaim Liberty ALL." Lying on the ground below it is a broken chain of slavery. (CA.)

On the morning of May 13, 1914, thousands of mourners silently passed the flag-draped caskets of two Philadelphia men who were among 17 American soldiers killed in Vera Cruz, Mexico. The bodies of Seamen George McKenzie Poinsett and Ordinary Seaman Charles Allen Smith lay in state in the Supreme Court Chamber of Independence Hall. Thirteen "bluejackets" and Marines from the Philadelphia Navy Yard stood guard as mourners paid their respects. (PH.)

The funeral procession of Seamen Poinsett and Smith is seen as it exits Independence Hall on May 13, 1914. The procession was attended by "the whole First Brigade of the National Guard of Pennsylvania, sailors and marines from the Navy Yard and scores of patriotic organizations as well as many officials," reported the *Philadelphia Record*. Thousands had lined the streets as the casket of each man was taken to its respective burial site. (PH.)

During World War I, the Liberty Bell took on a new role as a symbolic fundraiser. Liberty loans were government bonds used to support Allied forces during the war. The government recruited famous artists to design posters and Hollywood celebrities to host support rallies. This advertisement for the Third Liberty Loan was issued on April 5, 1918, and offered $3 billion in bonds at 4.5 percent interest. (FLP.)

The Liberty Bell is being removed from Independence Hall and hoisted onto a decorated flatbed truck in preparation for the Liberty Loan Parade on October 25, 1917. The parade was a promotion to stir patriotism among the citizens of Philadelphia to contribute financially toward the Allied forces during World War I. The Liberty Bell was the focal point of the parade, which traveled through the streets of the city. (INHP.)

The Liberty Bell is resting atop a beautifully decorated float in preparation for touring the streets of Philadelphia in the Liberty Loan Parade on October 25, 1917. The bell was accompanied by a costumed character dressed as Uncle Sam, who was the flag-bearer, and four men standing on the float with the bell in uniforms of former wars in the history of the United States. From left to right are the Revolutionary War, Civil War, Spanish-American War, and World War I. (INHP.)

The Human Liberty Bell was created by photographers Arthur Mole and John Thomas on June 20, 1918, from an 80-foot viewing tower using an 11-by-14 inch camera. They positioned 25,000 military men from Fort Dix, New Jersey, to form the image. The dimension from top to bottom was 580 feet. There are more than 11 times as many men in the beam as in the bell itself. (LC.)

"Commonwealth and City Pay Magnificent Tribute to Valorous Sons who Risked all in Liberty's Cause" read the headlines of the *Philadelphia Inquirer* on May 16, 1919. The parade, which took place the previous day, drew thousands along the route to welcome home the valiant heroes of World War I. The Pennsylvania 28th Iron Division marches past the Liberty Bell displayed outside Independence Hall as a tribute to their return. (CA.)

Mayor Thomas B. Smith of Philadelphia and Gov. William Cameron Sproul of Pennsylvania pose in front of the Liberty Bell at Independence Hall shortly after a wreath-laying ceremony on May 15, 1919. During a parade that honored Pennsylvania's returning men home from World War I, 67 wreathes were laid before the base of the bell representing each county in the Commonwealth of Pennsylvania in memory of their dead. (INHP.)

On September 12, 1919, Gen. John J. Pershing was honored in Philadelphia with possibly one of the largest parades the city had ever given to a war hero. The streets along the parade route were decorated with flowers and American flags. Even Independence Hall was adorned for the general's visit. Young ladies dressed in costumes representing each Allied nation that participated in World War I stand by the Liberty Bell. (INHP.)

General Pershing pays homage to the nation's symbol of freedom. An excerpt from the September 12, 1919, *Philadelphia Inquirer* reads, "With head bared and eyes softened, the man who had led the great army overseas to carry to victory the armed purpose that sprang into life in this historic shrine, riveted his eyes upon the Bell. He stood for a moment in silence and then straightened himself, [and] saluted." (INHP.)

The first two United States Marine honor guards to be assigned to stand guard next to the Liberty Bell during the nation's Sesquicentennial International Exposition in 1926 are seen here. Mayor W. Freeland Hendrick of Philadelphia requested the honor guard to dutifully stand at attention next to the historic relic during the hours Independence Hall was open to the public. A changing of the guard occurred every two hours, accompanied by a brief ceremony. (INHP.)

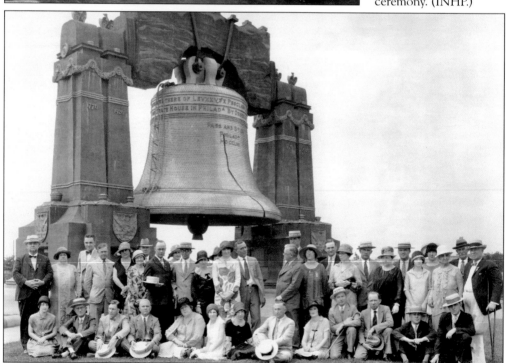

In 1926, Philadelphia held the Sesquicentennial International Exposition to celebrate the 150th anniversary of the United States. A replica of the Liberty Bell was constructed at what is present-day Marconi Plaza at Broad Street and Oregon Avenue and was tall enough to allow automobiles to pass beneath. The replica stood 80 feet tall and was lit at night by 26,000 lightbulbs. A group posed at the replica wearing hats reading '"Florida." (PH.)

Crowds gather in Independence Square on July 4, 1951, to celebrate the 175th anniversary of the signing of the Declaration of Independence. The daylong celebration began with a cast of 100 men, women, and children in costume reenacting the historic signing. Members of the Bell Ringers Association tolled out 1-7-7-6 in code on the tower bell, and Sen. James H. Duff of Pennsylvania delivered the keynote address. (INHP.)

Philadelphians celebrate the 175th anniversary of the signing of the Declaration of Independence on July 4, 1951. The celebration began with a parade that traveled from the Benjamin Franklin Parkway to Independence Hall. The parade consisted of 14 floats, 13 representing each original colony; 20 musical units; and marching units from the National Guard. The Pennsylvania float, seen here, portrayed the first public reading of the Declaration of Independence. (INHP.)

The "Woman's Liberty Bell," or the "Justice Bell," was inspired by Katharine Wentworth Ruschenberger of Strafford, Chester County, Pennsylvania, to symbolize liberty and justice for the women's suffrage movement. In 1915, she commissioned the Meneely Bell Company of Troy, New York, to create a replica of the Liberty Bell. Ruschenberger is quoted as saying, "The original Liberty Bell announced the creation of democracy; the Woman's Liberty Bell will announce the completion of democracy." The clapper was chained so that the bell could not toll until women were given the right to vote. In June 1915, the women began a three-month tour of Pennsylvania, stopping in every county in the commonwealth. A specially designed truck was created to transport the 2,000-pound bell. On August 18, 1920, the Nineteenth Amendment to the United States Constitution was ratified giving all citizens the right to vote regardless of sex. Today, the Woman's Liberty Bell is displayed in the Tower Room of the Washington Memorial Chapel in Valley Forge, Pennsylvania. (CA.)

On February 11, 1915, Mayor Rudolph Blankenburg of Philadelphia (far right) tapped the Liberty Bell three times with a wooden mallet as a symbolic gesture for the opening of the Panama-Pacific International Exposition in San Francisco. It was reported that the bell produced a dull muffled sound. In response, a replica of the Liberty Bell in San Francisco was tapped and the tone sent back to Philadelphia. (PH.)

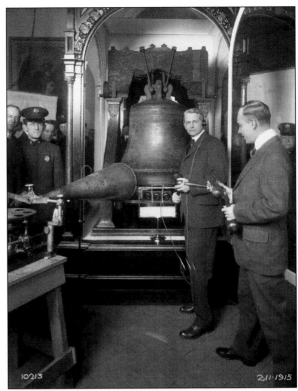

Mayor S. Davis Wilson of Philadelphia taps the Liberty Bell with a rubber mallet 11 times while World War I veterans look on to commemorate the 18th anniversary of the signing of the Allied and German armistice, which took place on the 11th hour of the 11th day of the 11th month in 1918. The tapping of the bell was simulcast over WFIL radio nationwide on November 11, 1936. (FLP.)

These newly naturalized Americans celebrate their first Fourth of July as citizens of the United States around the Liberty Bell in 1954. Seeking the American dream, millions have arrived in this country to enjoy a sense of newfound freedom and betterment of life. In that same year, Operation Wetback was put into place by the United States Immigration and Naturalization Service (INS) to remove illegal immigrants from the southwestern states. (CA.)

Benjamin Franklin assists two youngsters from the Girl and Boy Scouts of America to kick off a Keep America Beautiful campaign at Independence Hall on October 11, 1957. This program was sponsored by the Pittsburgh Jaycees and United States Steel Corporation. The Keep America Beautiful campaign was developed in 1953 to bring attention to the trash and litter along American highways and pollution released into the air and streams. (INHP.)

Jubilant residents of Juneau, Alaska, congregate around a replica of the Liberty Bell on June 30, 1958, after learning Alaska would soon become the 49th state. The Liberty Bell replica was one of 54 ordered by the United States Department of the Treasury to be cast by a foundry in France. Each state, territory, and the District of Columbia was given a bell to display and ring at patriotic occasions. (CA.)

Sen. Oren E. Long of Hawaii (center) is presented with a 50-star flag on July 4, 1960, which was flown over Independence Hall. The added star reflected Hawaii's admittance into the union the previous year. Participating in the ceremony were United States senators Hugh Scott (left) and Joseph S. Clark (right), both of Pennsylvania. (INHP.)

Astronaut Gus Grissom poses next to the capsule of *Liberty Bell 7* prior to its 15-minute space voyage on July 21, 1961. After the successful mission and splashdown, *Liberty Bell 7*'s hatch blew off mysteriously and sank to the bottom of the ocean. In 1999, the Discovery Channel helped retrieve the capsule. Today, *Liberty Bell 7* is on display at the Kansas Cosmosphere, an aerospace museum in Hutchinson, Kansas. (NASA.)

Posing with the Liberty Bell during Freedom Week in July 1962 are 11 youth, each born on July 4 and each from one of the original 13 colonies. Nicknamed Yankee Doodle Dandies, each youth wrote a composition theme "What My American Freedoms Mean to Me." Stephen Cybok Jr. (far left) won with his composition "Children's Declaration." (UA.)

On March 12, 1965, students from the University of Pennsylvania staged a sit-in around the base of the Liberty Bell. The students, representing a branch of the NAACP (National Association for the Advancement of Colored People) and the Student Non-Violent Coordinating Committee, walked into Independence Hall and began to sit on the floor around the bell. The students wore black armbands to protest the beating death of Rev. James J. Reeb, who was attacked by a mob of racists during a civil rights rally in Selma, Alabama. "We feel that this is a definite place that people look to when they think of freedom," commented Robert Brand, the student who led the sit-in. The students sat quietly; some even opened books to appear to study. During the sit-in, a group of schoolchildren from Gilbert Spruance Public School arrived for a tour. While explaining the history of the bell, tour guide Victoria F. Smith pointed out, "This," she said, "stands for liberty. There is nothing in the whole wide world anything [sic] more important now than liberty." (INHP.)

Blacks and whites gather together during a prayer vigil at Independence Hall, on March 14, 1965, in support of the civil rights marches in Selma, Alabama. Several people were injured and killed during the demonstrations, giving the first day of marches the nickname "Bloody Sunday." Images of Alabama law enforcement beating nonviolent protesters was shown around the world on television and newspapers, changing public opinion about the civil rights movement. (UA.)

Picketers march in front of Independence Hall in sub-freezing weather during a "freedom revival" rally on March 20, 1967. Nearly 100 people rallied in support of the unfair treatment of African Americans in the labor field. The protest was led by Cecil B. Moore, president of the Philadelphia Chapter of the NAACP. (UA.)

Protesters against the United States' involvement in Vietnam demonstrate in front of Independence Hall on July 4, 1967. Many of the protesters were members of Veterans for Peace in Vietnam. Young adults in America were the biggest opponents of the war, staging protests on college campuses. Network news commentaries brought the war into America's living rooms nightly. The United States' involvement in Vietnam would end in August 1973. (UA.)

Anti-Vietnam veterans carry a replica of the Liberty Bell in front of Independence Hall during an antiwar movement rally on December 29, 1971. The veterans and students were joined by 225 scientists who were attending a conference in Philadelphia. Veterans who were leading then began to chant "Bring 'em home, bring our brothers home." The rally was sparked by renewed bombing in North Vietnam by the American military. (UA.)

111

Gay rights demonstrations, known as "Annual Reminder Day Pickets," took place each July 4 from 1965 to 1969. In this 1966 rally, picketers emphasized that gay Americans were denied the rights of "life, liberty, and the pursuit of happiness" guaranteed by the Declaration of Independence. The marches were commemorated in 2005 with the placement of a historical marker by the Pennsylvania Historical and Museum Commission at Sixth and Chestnut Streets. (CA.)

Mayor William J. Green III of Philadelphia stands at the podium with the Liberty Bell Pavilion in the background during an interdenominational prayer service on January 22, 1981. The 30-minute service was held in celebration of the release of 52 Americans held hostage in Tehran, Iran, for 444 days. The crisis, which began in November 1979, ended January 1981, just minutes after Ronald Reagan was sworn into office. (INHP.)

Seven

VISITING THE ICONS OF DEMOCRACY

As a tourist attraction, Independence Hall and the Liberty Bell have attracted visitors for over a century. Author Charlene Mires notes in her book *Independence Hall: in American Memory* that attendance increased in the 1960s and 1970s. Recent reports show visitation to the park number over two million per year. Here, groups of schoolchildren gather in the square for an orientation lecture by a park ranger in 1952. (INHP.)

In 1951, during the 175th anniversary of the signing of the Declaration of Independence, many Americans found a renewed sense of patriotism and pride. Visitors were drawn to Independence Hall and the Liberty Bell to reconnect with America's heritage. National Park Service ranger and historian Robert Trawny gives a lecture about the Liberty Bell. (INHP.)

Students from Upper Darby High School visited Independence Hall on November 22, 1955. Independence Hall and the Liberty Bell continue to be a primary location for visits from school students and teachers. From September until May, young people of all grade levels find visiting these historic icons stimulating to their studies. (INHP.)

On June 14, 1961, radio and television personality Arthur Godfrey was presented with a plaque by Frank Fruscott. Fans and spectators surround Godfrey during the presentation with the Liberty Bell behind him. Godfrey became a public favorite from his radio and television programs. Celebrities like Pat Boone, Patsy Cline, and Steve Allen received their fame from appearing on one of Godfrey's shows. (INHP.)

The Reverend Dr. Billy Graham (right) and John Robinson of Altoona, Pennsylvania (left), inspect the underside of the Liberty Bell during the filming of a television documentary titled *The World of Billy Graham*. Reverend Graham brought his famous crusade to Philadelphia in November 1961. He preached before thousands at the Philadelphia Convention Center and visited a local state correctional institution. (INHP.)

Philadelphia native astronaut Charles "Pete" Conrad Jr. (center) stands between Mayor James Tate (right) and Independence National Historical Park superintendent Melford O. Anderson (left) on October 12, 1965. Commander Conrad was given a ticker tape parade through the city. Conrad received the Philadelphia Medal of Honor, the city's highest decoration. Astronaut Conrad spent eight days in space on *Gemini 5*'s orbital flight in August 1965. (INHP.)

Television talk show host Dinah Shore stands with Mayor Frank Rizzo next to the Liberty Bell in March 1973. The mayor was a special guest on Shore's syndicated talk show called *Dinah's Place*, which aired from 1970 to 1974. The mayor presented Shore with the Honorary Citizen Citation and the Philadelphia Bowl. The episode aired on May 29, 1973, with Dinah singing "Philadelphia With Love." (PH.)

Comedian Bob Hope (right) admires the Liberty Bell along with Mayor Frank Rizzo (left) and actor Joel Grey (center) on July 4, 1975. Hope became the third American to receive the Philadelphia Freedom Medal. Mayor Rizzo commented that Hope is "a true humanitarian" who "has earned his place among the immortals." During the ceremony, Joel Grey read the Declaration of Independence and the Liberty Bell was symbolically tapped. (PH.)

Singer and actor Frank Sinatra receives the Philadelphia Freedom Medal from Mayor Frank Rizzo on July 4, 1977. The mayor expressed that the medal was honoring Sinatra for "exemplifying American ideals" and "perpetuating the American heritage." After accepting the award, Sinatra hoped that his success story would serve as an inspiration to young people, that "a poor kid from the other side of the tracks can make it." (PH.)

On his first visit to Philadelphia, His Holiness the 14th Dalai Lama, whose real name is Tenzin Gyatso, gives the peace sign while standing next to the Liberty Bell on September 22, 1990. Standing with him is Hobart G. Cawood, superintendent of the Independence National Historical Park. Surprised that the Liberty Bell was cracked, the Dalai Lama was heard later to say, "I believe this is a reminder to American people—who enjoy so much freedom in this country—that in other parts of the world . . . there is no freedom. You cannot be truly free if not everybody is free." Winner of the 1989 Nobel Peace Prize, the Dalai Lama's visit was part of a three-week tour of North America. His main mission to the "City of Brotherly Love" was to participate in the 250th anniversary of the founding of the University of Pennsylvania. He spoke to an audience at the university's Irvine Auditorium. (INHP.)

Civil rights leader Rev. Dr. Martin Luther King Jr. stands beside the Liberty Bell along with Dr. Emanuel C. Wright, president of the National Freedom Day Association, on February 1, 1959. The men laid a wreath at the foot of the bell on the 18th Freedom Day observance commemorating the adoption of the 13th Amendment prohibiting slavery. During Dr. King's visit, he spoke about the peaceful integration of schools in Virginia. (PH.)

In a symbolic striking of the Liberty Bell on January 18, 1988, civil rights activist Rosa Parks joins Mayor W. Wilson Goode of Philadelphia in celebration of the birthday of the late Dr. Martin Luther King Jr. The striking occurred simultaneously with bells in Atlanta and London. The ceremony was part of daylong activities to celebrate Martin Luther King Jr. Day, which was first observed in the United States on January 20, 1986. (UPI.)

On February 22, 1861, president-elect Abraham Lincoln addressed a crowd at Independence Hall, marking the 129th anniversary of George Washington's birth. This was one of several inaugural stops Lincoln would make before advancing to Washington, D.C., prior to taking the presidential oath. A six-foot-high wooden platform was constructed between Independence Hall and Chestnut Street. The platform was decorated with large American flags on all sides. Lincoln stood and addressed the crowd: "I have often inquired of myself, what great principle or idea it was that kept this Confederacy so long together. It was not the mere matter of the separation of the colonies from the mother land; but something in that Declaration giving liberty, not alone to the people of this country, but hope to the world for all future time." A flag-raising ceremony also took place. Kansas had just been admitted to the Union as a free state on January 29. President-elect Lincoln was given the honor of raising the new 34-star flag high above Independence Hall. As the flag unfurled, the crowd cheered and the band played "The Star-Spangled Banner." (ALPLM.)

During a campaign visit to Philadelphia, Republican candidate Gen. Dwight D. Eisenhower and wife Mamie took the opportunity to visit Independence Hall on September 4, 1952. Seen here, the general and his wife sign the guest book in the Supreme Court Chamber. The *Philadelphia Inquirer* reported that while General Eisenhower gazed upon the Liberty Bell, "His face was sober as he gently touched the bell, completely oblivious for a moment." (INHP.)

Pres. John F. Kennedy stands before the Liberty Bell with Mayor James Tate of Philadelphia on July 4, 1962. Kennedy addressed a crowd of 100,000 people and stated that "[the] doctrine of national independence has shaken the globe, and it remains the most powerful force anywhere in the world today. The theory of independence . . . was not invented in this hall, but it was in this hall that the theory became a practice." (PH.)

During Freedom Week of July 4, 1963, Vice Pres. Lyndon B. Johnson and wife Lady Bird visited Philadelphia. Johnson spoke about the challenges of civil rights, commenting that if an American can be ordered by the president to sit in a foxhole during wartime, that same American has the right to enter a "hamburger stand, a toilet, or a movie theater without harassment." After his speech, Johnson visited the Liberty Bell. (INHP.)

Pres. Richard M. Nixon uses Independence Hall as a backdrop to sign the Revenue Sharing Act on October 20, 1972. The bill faced strong opposition in Congress. It would allocate $30 billion over five years to state and local governments according to a formula based on relative populations and incomes. It would have little direct impact on rural development programs. Standing behind Nixon is Vice Pres. Spiro Agnew, fourth from left. (PH.)

Celebrating America's bicentennial, Pres. Gerald Ford addressed a crowd of over 100,000 in front of Independence Hall on July 4, 1976. The president stated how humbling it was to stand before an iconic piece of American history. Sharing the platform that morning were actor Charlton Heston, Gov. Milton Shapp of Pennsylvania, noted contralto Marian Anderson, and Archbishop Iakovos of the Greek Orthodox Church of North and South America. (GFL.)

On April 1, 1987, Pres. Ronald Reagan spoke to volunteers and staff of We the People, an organization created to prepare for the 200th anniversary of the United States Constitution. T.L. Davies of Independence National Historical Park photographed the president speaking in the House of Representatives Chamber of Congress Hall. In 1988, Reagan signed the Constitution Heritage Act providing for the construction of the National Constitution Center. (INHP.)

The Korean Children's Choir posed around the Liberty Bell on April 22, 1954, as they visited Independence Hall. The choir, sponsored by the American-Korean Foundation, arrived in the United States on a nationwide tour to help aid their country after the Korean War. Brig. Gen. Crawford F. Sams, one of the United States Army's highest ranking doctors during the Korean Conflict, stands among the children in the second row, far right. (INHP.)

Dignitaries from Ghana assemble in Independence Hall in front of the Liberty Bell to celebrate Ghana Independence Day in this March 6, 1957, photograph taken by W.A. McCullough. The Gold Coast gained its independence from Great Britain that year and was renamed Ghana after the Empire of Ghana. The new nation was the first sub-Saharan African nation to achieve its independence from Great Britain. (INHP.)

Prime Minister Mohammed Mossadegh of Iran sits in the Rising Sun Chair as he signs the guest registry book in the Assembly Room of Independence Hall on October 22, 1951. The prime minister entered office on April 28, 1951, and was ousted in a coup on August 19, 1953. The coup was organized by the CIA and the British M16. (INHP.)

On July 6, 1976, Her Majesty Queen Elizabeth II of Great Britain and Prince Philip gaze upon the Liberty Bell during their six-day bicentennial tour of the United States. The queen, the first reigning British monarch to visit Philadelphia, was heard to say as she walked around the bell, "You know this is one of the finest symbols of any country in the world. Everyone knows about the Liberty Bell." (INHP.)

Chancellor Helmut Schmidt of West Germany visited Philadelphia on a bicentennial courtesy call on July 17, 1976. Schmidt, who served as chancellor of West Germany from 1974 to 1982, arrived in Philadelphia for a three-hour visit. The purpose of his trip was to "thank the people of America for what they did for us after World War II." During a visit to the Liberty Bell, Schmidt tapped bell with his knuckles. (INHP.)

Pres. Raúl Alfonsin of Argentina tours the Assembly Room in Independence Hall with Supt. Hobart G. Cawood of Independence National Historical Park on June 19, 1987, in celebration of the 200th anniversary of the United States Constitution. Alfonsin was the first democratically elected president of Argentina following a military government from 1983 to 1989. While in Philadelphia, he addressed a meeting of the World Affairs Council and the Philadelphia Bar Association. (INHP.)

In May 1988, Prime Minister Harri Holkeri of Finland and wife Marja-Liisa Lepisto visited Philadelphia to open an exhibit at the Port of History Museum celebrating the 350th anniversary of the first Finnish settlement in America. Supt. Hobart G. Cawood points to the inscription on the Liberty Bell while Mayor W. Wilson Goode (left), Mrs. Holkeri (center), and the prime minister look on. (INHP.)

Supt. Hobart C. Cawood points out the Rising Sun Chair used by George Washington during the Constitutional Convention to the Polish politician and cofounder of Solidarity trade-union movement, Lech Walesa. Walesa became the first recipient of the Liberty Medal, which was awarded him on July 4, 1989. Speaking before the crowd, Walesa said the medal "symbolized the link between democracy and Solidarity, a link best described as freedom." (INHP.)

DISCOVER THOUSANDS OF LOCAL HISTORY BOOKS FEATURING MILLIONS OF VINTAGE IMAGES

Arcadia Publishing, the leading local history publisher in the United States, is committed to making history accessible and meaningful through publishing books that celebrate and preserve the heritage of America's people and places.

Find more books like this at
www.arcadiapublishing.com

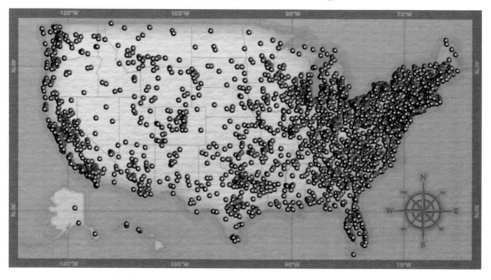

Search for your hometown history, your old stomping grounds, and even your favorite sports team.